rebel for love

# REBEL FOR LOVE

## Kaileia É. M. Suvannamaccha

HEARTFUL EVOLUTION

*for the woman who dares to love.*
*may we remember each time we forget*
*that, in love, all of us always belongs.*

REBELS, ENTER HERE.

# THERE IS NO TRIGGER WARNING FOR LIFE.

the mother's water breaks,
the fetus—unprepared
for the loss of our first home

but as our lungs expand,
so does our world
and with it, the awareness

that the greatest gift
is only ever borrowed,
comes with strings
that tie us to our angel wings,
leading us through the unknown

with no guarantees
except that
the last loss
we'll ever face
will be our own.

kaileia suvannamaccha

# HE KILLED THE POETRY

by placing his hand
where my pen used to be.

he killed the poetry
by filling my head with now moments
instead of repeating memories.

he killed the poetry
by becoming it,
by loving me

now
now
now.

# HE LEFT ME

on the back burner
indefinitely.

he left me
after I asked him not to walk so far ahead,
rather
just walk beside me.

he left me
in Whole Foods with no wallet,
no phone,
no other mode of transportation to get home.

now I'm crying at blurry price tags and food labels
of snacks I am no longer hungry for
because I am too full of sadness,
of grief,
of the hole that's been carved from my own chest.
I'm not breathing anymore because
he left me.

I'm not breathing because I'm holding
onto his backpack, refusing
to wrap my arms
around him—

tell him *I'd rather fall*
and pray I do,
off the back of his motorcycle

and just lay there,
lifeless on the pavement
and wonder then
if he would even think
to turn around—

corners of my mouth drooping in the wind
between child-like whimpers
from the old woman I've become
over years spent waiting
for him—a man
who,
when I needed him the most,
left me

alone
in the nights I wanted him
though I couldn't have him,
or when I did, that having him felt
more like having a ghost, so
*I might as well be dead*
I said—in my head,
still crying at the thought of letting go.

undoing the single strap of my helmet,
now I can really imagine
what it might feel like
to fall—helpless,
brain juice leaking out
all over the path
his daily tires trek,
taking him to and from empty places

because the one that's already so full of him
is never enough,
so he must seek
that which runs out.

*so sick*
I think, that maybe if
I let my heart bleed out,
could that be what it takes
for him to stay, for once?

to finally see
the steps he might wish to retrace,
or maybe,
just maybe
at least have the thought cross his mind
that maybe he shouldn't have
left me
in the first place?

yet in the end,
all that's left
is this heart, still beating
as I reflect and express
through art, the feelings I felt
those nights that
he left me—
all that's left

me.

# FORGET-ME-NOT

I am lonely
in all of the places
you forgot to look for me—

in the frizz of my locks
where the waves should be,

in the lava-filled craters
of this mask called skin,

in the chaos of my monkey mind
that keeps me buried beneath layers of blanket,

in the fire of my womb
that only seems to ignite
once pain drips, lines my cheeks,
and my lungs are weak
and my throat has turned to desert—

all this you miss
every time you say *I love you*
to a woman you don't even know
because you forget
to take a closer look
at the heart
that's melting
right in front of you.

# DEAR LOVER,

when did it stop being fun?

when was the last time you teared up
thinking about us?

when did you start feeling tired?

when did your passion and burning desire
fade into a ghostly presence
that I have to beg to keep,
let alone to faintly see?

tell me why a screen is more mesmerizing
than my eyes, and why
then, do you still fail to see
the words I send you,
and remember to respond without my asking of you?

because I remember a time when I didn't have to.

a time when I could speak
and you'd keep your eyes locked on mine,
a time where time spent together meant more
than two bodies laying side by side,
a feeling that made me thankful
every other love I had died

because there was more room for you
because your love was like mine—deep and true

and now
it seems the only way you
love me,
you don't even mean to.

you don't need to

because once you get the prize,
there's always something bigger out there
to pursue,

so I guess that's all I was to you.

it's not what I thought it'd be,
not even close.
it's not how you promised me,
not what I chose.
I was under the impression
my asking of questions
would take me closer to truth—
closer to you
but all I ever got close to
were the lies
you left behind you.

*you're my favorite toy*
*and I'll never grow up.*
what does that mean?
I ask him, hopeful.
*it means I'll never stop*
*playing with you.*

come on gut,
you gotta let me keep him.
this one I may not trust
but I still want to
believe him.

## QUIET TEARS

a theme in my life is this scene—
I'm laying in bed beside him
and can't quite figure out
which part of me feels
repressed,
numb,
or lost,
and though I try to rewrite it
each time it plays,
I can never speak in time.
I can never let him in my mind
because sorting through feelings,
I still can't find
the pieces of me I'm missing.
why can't I let myself sing?
could it be that
the voice carries the soul
and that is far
too precious of a thing?

inside this cocoon,
there is room for two.
allow it to envelop you,
see behind the scenes.
it is a privilege to preview
the unbecoming
before the emergence
of wings.

kaileia suvannamaccha

## DAWN'S RECITAL

I am free in the dark
of one thousand shifting faces
invisible to the eye
yet nostalgic to the ear—
a symphony of memories.

none last long
as the tears that follow
or the race in my brain
paralyzing me in sorrow.

I need evidence
to support these claims
so I search the unbroken sky
for a hint of truth
that I might feel
to color in

but if this moment passes
before I can grasp it,
all is lost—I am lost
in every puddle I ever stepped in.

birdsong, wake me from this nightmare.
take me back to the world of dreams.
blanket me in a faint remembrance
of time—with no end.

## BUDDHA IS NO LOVE EXPERT

tell Buddha I've attached to my attachments.
I want the man six feet under me,
making graves of each other's hearts
to forever reside in
while we're still living.

tell him I stop eating
when my heart is sick to its stomach
and shrinks to the size that I feel
when my love support is unplugged
by the one who promised to help water the garden,
promised he loved every flower just as I did
and wouldn't pluck them
like I do, his scattered back hairs.

tell Buddha I'm drunk on love,
dancing with the demon of attachment,
cheek to cheek, inhaling the musky scent
of his sweat and pheromones,
fingers tracing the landscape
with a hand that grips like thunder,
shakes the hills,
skinny-dips then dives into crevasses,
unearthing red-hot magma and salty-sweet sea spray
between word vomiting on each other
just to kiss every wound after
eye to eye to eye to eye
holding
and not wanting to let go
ever. ever. ever.

and after,
tell the true story—
Buddha abandoned his princess,
left the seed born of their love that he planted in her,
left her to water it alone—
that which their love made in his image
to immortalize his own.

my heart still breaks for her.

how to lay beside a warm body,
then learn to fall asleep without one?
how to wake without his morning breath on her face
after taking him into the depths of her?
how to love, really love, and let love in
without making a home there?

tell Buddha
loving without attachment
is the real sin.

# EAT UP, GIRL!

what love are you in
if you leave yourself out?

does hope still float
when you drown it in doubt?

whenever waves crash,
even they retreat from shore.

do you fail to eat your fill
'cause you're so used to wanting more?

if silence spoke a thousand words,
you wouldn't hesitate

to leave the one who left your heart
upon their dinner plate

warm,
wet,
still beating—

what a waste.

# THE LOVE YOU WITHHOLD IS WASTED

hop on the back of his motorcycle barefoot.
buy her local orchids that smell like chocolate
just because.
put your life in the hands of another,
then jump
out of the plane.

don't ask if it's a good idea.
ask if it makes you feel alive!
tell the old flame you still burn for them.

call your mom on a May Wednesday at 2:32 pm.
keep her on Facetime
while you're in the shower
and she's on the toilet.

dive into the ice cream bin
with the same enthusiasm
as you did (or didn't) the salad bowl.

taste test every part of the body
(at least once).
let your skin stretch and sag
the way it was made to.

duet with a stranger at karaoke.
stare into the eyes of your greatest enemy,
then, kiss the mirror.

live immediately
like Seneca,
whose life was long
since he knew how to live it.

I know
this life is long,
as long as you love it

and
all the love you withhold
is love wasted.

## ROSE & IVY

tonight, I chose me.
coconut pineapple siesta key
rum, and I don't even drink
but I'd rather
savor this flavor—
try something new
than lay in bed waiting for you.
each sip takes me to
crystal sand-decorated toes.
tonight, main character energy looks like
dining alone,
only checking my phone
for directions.
it was never my responsibility
to fix your misunderstanding of me.

*but how can you love something*
*you don't understand?*
I ask.
*sometimes,* he says.
*that's why you love it.*

you had a fire in your eyes.
it burned when you stared in mine.
neither of my hands were tied
but I was tired, deep inside.
thought you wanted us to survive?
I still don't know how
I made it out alive.

## STITCHES

this heart
splits right down the middle
when we fight.
I feel the rift
and I'm the only one
who thinks
to bring out the stitches,
but you just rip it open,
let it all bleed out,
take your half and run with it,
and leave me
to chase you
with mine.

## TINY RAZORS

eyes puffed to perfection.
is that the only way you want me?
if it isn't, I can't tell
because you only lay your hand upon my heart
when it's hurting,
once I tell you I stopped breathing
and I wonder, if I ever let you leave me,
that you would stay gone,
but I don't know
how not to beg.
I don't know
how not to
want to be fed,
so I put the treats in your hand,
open my mouth
and kneel,
still starving,
and the couch is starting to feel
a little less like running away,
a little more like a place
where my heart is finally safe
from the words you don't mean
but you say anyway—
tiny razors in my throat,
so tiny I can't choke,
but that doesn't mean
I'm not still bleeding
on the inside.

# HEAR HER

stop begging him—
the one who listens with half a brain.

the mirror is covered.
it doesn't let light in,
and you expect a reflection?

sometimes, all a woman needs is to listen,
to really hear herself
and tell herself—out loud,

*I'm listening to you.*
*I've been listening to you.*
*I'll remind you of this when you need me to.*

*you expressed how you felt*
*and you held space for him,*
*even when he couldn't do the same for you.*

*I'm so proud of you*
*for speaking your truth,*
*for not making his incapacity to be there*
*about you.*

*and, for what it's worth—*
*and it's worth everything,*
*I know your worth*
*and I'll always be here for you.*

when love is the frontier,
you can choose to be a settler
or a pioneer.

## LOVE BEYOND THE FRONTIER

I am not a settler.
I am a pioneer.
the love I seek is seeking me
and there are no rings here.

no fancy houses to feign safety or security,
no beds to lazily lay in—so cozy
just to wake up one day and realize
we are not the same.

I keep myself hungry—
for in hunger,
I find an insatiable appetite
and will not fill this belly
(for my worth is measured
in more than eggs).

I need me a cowboy—
one who doesn't live the same day to day.
all that's his changes as he does
and he likes it that way,
as do I.

I want a love that comes
and comes again.
this isn't a one-and-done,
slip in, slip out—or not, kind of thing.

in this life, there will be lots and lots of love
to fall in

all over again—
each day, in a new way
in a new place
to a new person
because we are never the same.

Heraclitus said it best
about the rivers
but he left out the part
about rivers leading back
to an ocean—that all-inclusive love fest

but a river must travel
else it becomes stagnant,
else it dries up if it can't take the spotlight,
else it is polluted by the unnatural things
that fill its belly,
leaving no room
for hunger,
for desire—

else it forgets
it was a teardrop from the gods
to begin.

on my darkest days,
in my hardest moments,
the love of strangers has held me
where others would have family
or friends
or lovers.
I am grateful for the love
that finds me
wherever I am.

## TONIGHT,

I teared up in the arms of a waitress, who
moved a mountain to reunite with her daughter, who
ended up in the foster care system for five years
because of a man, who
didn't know how to care for either.

tonight, I fell asleep
on the beach during sunset,
wrapped in a wet towel—
a butterfly in my cocoon
after a long day of tears.

tonight, the ocean held me,
my own salt water mixing
with that which makes up
Mother Nature's womb.

she held me,
rocked me gently
to the lullaby of her waves, and
as I let the water run across my eyelids,
I could still see
the glistening reflection of sunlight.

tonight, I wore a hand-me-down dress that
once belonged to my second cousin, that
I cut to fit my 5'2" petite frame.

I walked downtown until I found
the restaurant that felt right

and ate a meal custom-picked for my blood type—
blackened salmon and caesar salad,
a strawberry faux-jito,
and tiramisu.

tonight, I met a sheriff, who
spoke love over me,
sang and danced
(he was off-duty).
we bonded over our love for animals, while
he and his childhood best friend smiled
genuine smiles

and laughed.
we all laughed
and spoke all the good things
about Tom Cruise
and Hawaii
and then, he paid for me.

tonight, had I chosen
not to care for my little princess,
I would have missed out
on the magic
that comes with
living fully alive

but since I did, now,
at the end of it all,
I get to reflect
on everything I have survived.

let me taste the heart of who you are—
the sweetness of your innocence,
the bitterness of your scars.

pain & pleasure
are two sides of the same coin like

nervousness                    excitement
creation                          destruction
loving                              hating
living                               dying

the pendulum must swing
or we are left with

nothing

I can't think of anything more worth living for.
those who say there is haven't loved like this, I'm sure.

## DIVINE LOVING

before you judge your lover,
speak to them like they are your God
(and not the God that punishes).

the God that loves unconditionally,
that sends you signs before you ask
even when you can't understand them yet.

the God you marvel at
wherever you see beauty
and whenever you feel love.

the God you thank
for your hard-earned blessings,
that make the hard-learned lessons
make that much more sense.

the God you rely on
to land the plane, clear the path,
to make it through this life and death.

the God you swore you wouldn't believe in
but now, somehow, can never forget.

## ANGEL WINGS

my merman and I
crack open a sand dollar,
make wishes on the doves,
wonder if there are angel wings
inside all of us.

float upon, then body surf
the tenderly folding waves,
come home to read a book in bed,
my thighs around his face.

flip the pages, switch positions
'til the candle is ready and hot,
then a trail of rose oil down my spine—
a massage reserved for gods.

we seal it with a soft lip,
open-mouth kiss,
sloping down the neck
until the air becomes thick.

my merman, then,
grips my waist, pulls me in,
and just like that, we're back
in an ocean, once again.

## LULLABY

in your arms, I could die—satisfied.
I'm only afraid when we aren't together,
afraid of lightning and thunder,
body-heat-less nights,
a world of darkness without your light,
remembering the ghost of you
and the flames we trained to ignite.
so when the time comes—as it must,
let us promise to leave together
so neither of us will have to suffer
through too-long years of reminders
of the missing heartbeat,
that music to the ear upon the chest,
the only lullaby we'll ever need.

kaileia suvannamaccha

## WHY MUSES ARE SUCH INSOMNIACS

the subconscious is the submarine
that swims through the unconscious sea
running deep below
the conscious living we experience.
these worlds coexist,
but one is always reflected.
as we mirror what goes on
within and down under,
the muses find room
to hide, play, and party on,
even as we slumber.

## MY DREAM

your love is like a prayer—the only one I need.
it contains all that I long for
and all I wish to keep.

my love paints you as a God
as you unchain me from my demons
while the Devil in you makes love
to every facet of my being,

simultaneously freeing me
as you're making me yours.
I devote each breath to you,
my precious life force.

there's no life without loving
and I've loved, but not like this.
you—my God, my love,
breaking waves in my ocean,

make rain fall, then evaporate,
brewing up our love potion.
it's because you give me pleasure
that you can also bring me pain.

they are but two sides of the same
coin that every day, I choose to invest,
wishing for nothing else
but to lay upon your chest—
and rest, not just sleep,

in hopes to wake again
and remember
that you are
and you've always been
my dream.

maybe death
is just waking up
from the dream that is life.

# MIRAGE

when you walk in the city at night,
you'll likely find
more stars in asphalt than in sky,
and when the light
hits it just right,
you just might
wish
that what you see
is just a dream
and not the reality.

## LIVING THINGS

in another world,
I am the mother
who gets the procedure.

my uterus is swapped out
for one that works better
so I can be the first
to successfully deliver
three. goat. kids.
one after the other.

it's breakthrough technology!
new, innovative IVF
and no one blinks an eye
because this sort of thing
happens all the time.

instead of mutant robots,
we save endangered species!
raise them wild
without expectation
for them to do anything
but be everything
they already are,

and the stars
are not
where wishes go to waste
on shiny things
in sky or on screen.

kaileia suvannamaccha

they are in the field—
green,
giving birth
to living things.

in a world where body mutilation has become
normalized, it has become an act of rebellion
to live as nature intended.

# TAN LINES

you should know my ass
has never seen the light of day
and up until the first time I got braids,
neither had my scalp.

unlike you,
I don't have the privilege
of walking down the street,
working out,
sunbathing at the beach, or even
lounging on the couch
without covering my chest
(all because I've got a little more flesh).

you should know
that for me, it's the little things,
that if my outside matched my inside
and if I were truly free,
I would lose these lines in a fortress of forest,
dancing with my own shadow.

so for now, I need you to kiss me
a little longer on these parts,
make me feel like gold on your tongue
since these parts don't get kissed
a whole lot by the sun.

this lonely captivity
replays in the mind,
stealing breath
with every memory,
praying they leave
as he did.

# NAÏVETÉ

there was a love I felt when I was young—
unreserved, just free and fun,
a love I had for only one
that I was sure of

but I mistook him for the sun
not knowing he was water,
or that water doesn't stay—it flows,
and therefore, he would need to go

and though I knew we couldn't burn,
I trusted that he would return
so when he didn't,
I had to learn

that tides change, shells remain,
and birds still sing their songs
for those who will listen,

soaring above the shore,
uncertain of what for,
but always wishing,

wanting

more.

love, like memories,
cannot be replaced,
only added to.

## WHAT IF

I've got more love to give?
not just one or two,
nor me and you,
but three or four
or more,
and I love you all
in a different way.
not every love must look the same
(or feels the same).
must love be limited
when love is infinite?
and we are all one life
like the sun is one light
until day becomes night
and even dead stars shine bright,
and somewhere,
on the other side of the planet,
the same sun gives birth to new life.
a new day has begun—
another chance for love
to be given or taken,
for those asleep to awaken,
and all the while,
more love than I can count
is being made.

once you have to catch yourself,
you forget how to let go.

# MY OLD NAME BELONGS TO YOU.

you,
the only one who could say it
lovingly enough.

your accent,
that mountain view,
the first morning waking up next to you.

on the train,
as your fingers made their way up and into
my heart
as we made our way through
the city for the day

and on the way back
that night, I cried
because part of me knew
it was the last time I'd ever see you.

goodbye arcade, goodbye mountain view
goodbye city streets, ninja feasts,
and long car rides with you,
ice cream parking lot love-making,
nature walks and talks,

and the name I always hated,
that I only loved because of
you.

## FLOUNDERING

I am a little mermaid, but one you can't keep.
I come in waves and must slip away
but you will always remember

my heart, like love,
does not know any other.

this time, my cup
does not run out,
only runneth over

so much that I sense you
in the silence of the night.

I still see you in my dreams,
in ways not so innocent
as waking life.

if only to relate didn't mean possession,
I might have even
belonged
to you both.

## MEMENTO

through the window of a moving train,
I watch whole worlds pass me by—
worlds that will go unexplored.

perhaps,
we weren't meant to cling or dive,
but for a moment—a fragment,
only within we are truly alive.

perhaps,
it is our presence we ought to count,
not just the time.

I'm not innocent.
I have my demons too
but what a relief it is
to share my stories
and still be loved by you.

I just want to see
if I can make you love
everything you think you hate

so when you tell me
you don't like red lipstick
today,

you already know
what I'll be kissing you in
tomorrow.

## L'ADIEU

my heart led me to you,
a painting worth melting into.
I followed the thread we tossed—
yarn that wound itself across the earth,
kept me tethered to a moment in time,
an unexplored potential.
perhaps, we were better as a fantasy.
perhaps, we weave clothing out of knotted thread
to protect our most vulnerable parts—our hearts
that know not of any other,
know not of sweat-stained sheets,
city lights, or regrets
from fire left untamed,
know only of desire
to connect.
the mind isn't so innocent
but the body knows its secrets—
trading cards of memories
though it cannot show its hand,
only play it.

if you tell her
you're afraid of the ocean,
you're also telling her
you're scared of
what makes up
most of what you are.

## BEFORE THE STORM

waves are a force
but water is stronger.
deep down under,
it is still
calmer.
the sound of the ocean can soothe you.
a hug from a wave can comfort you,
but do not underestimate it.
please, do not be mistaken.
it can lift you high,
then pull you down.
you can float
and you can drown
when water flows in
and all around.

I feel her feeling
and will not ask her to be
less of what she is.

## ROXANNE'S POV

I'm not sorry
for the way his lips felt on mine
or the wetness between my thighs,
his whispering French in my ear,
and if I could do it all again,
I'd let him take me from behind,

but only in the jungle—
wild, raw sex.
no need to question if I'm wanted,
I won't beg.

if only his moans didn't sound like squeals,
if only his sweat was as fragrant as yours.

I waited
to hear your low growl,
to feel your hard strokes.

I wanted
the thick of him with your length.
his words, your image

since I never get
wet like that
for you,
I thought I was broken
but it was just
all these words left unspoken
between us.

each vowel, heat for my soul
so when we finally touch,
we're stoking a fire,
not just rubbing two sticks together.

ha! but what really is there
to like in a man
besides his penis?
even then, do we like him
or just envy his freedom?

## THE BODY IS A MORE DISCIPLINED LOVER.

heart wisdom is inclusive—
it knows no other!
each time the heart breaks,
it only opens wider.
the heart is a survivalist,
can find love in every place,
fall in love with any face.
that feeling—full of love
creates infinite space.

the body, however,
has a wisdom all its own.
it's more discerning with
the territory it calls home.
selective with what information
it chooses to carry,
generations of memories remain,
albethey long-buried.

so when a woman's heart lurks
into dangerous zones,
her body will detect it first
and try to let her know.
whether or not she listens
will depend on her awareness,
regardless of how obvious
her symptoms prove apparent.

# IT'S A MAN'S WORLD AFTER ALL!

all men know
is how to work
but all I want to do
is play

so,
*play with me*
I say

but no,
I have to wait
to work
to get a man to play.

*this isn't the way*
*we, women,*
*were made*
I wait
to say

because now,
I have to work
to pay
to play.

oh, are we playing a game? I suck at all games.
*well, you can't suck at this game.*
actually, I suck the most at this game.
*it's life.*
exactly. I especially suck at that one.
*you can't. it's just luck.*

in life, you get to decide
which parts of you get to live
and which parts need to die
but if you don't choose,
you might lose
the best of you
to the worst of you,
or worse—to the worst of someone else
who forgot they had the power to choose.

## WHEN THE PAPER IS MORE PATIENT
*after Anne Frank*

I never thought of myself as quiet.
my thoughts are always on.
when someone comments on my shyness,
they haven't visited my mind.
they don't know
it is already
so loud.

# I DON'T WRITE HAPPY POEMS.

I write the truth as I feel it.
I write the pain as I heal it,
so if you're old
and in need of a happy story told,
by now, you ought to have lived it yourself
'cause when you pick up my book from the shelf,
and read it,
and realize
it's exactly what you needed,
you'll know it,
even if you refuse to admit it
out loud.

# DEAR ARTIST,

did you forget you are the creator?
did you forget how to let love in?
how to let it come through
and pour out into
something—
bigger than you?

you are not the art, artist.
you are not the masterpiece.
you are a work in progress 'til the very end, so
watch what you say and how you speak.

did you forget how to respect
your muse? your inspiration?
your reason? your dedication?
your purpose? your mission?
treating the ones you love like a means to an end
when we are the fuel for your very pen,
paintbrush, or instrument?

do you remember how to play
with care, cleverness, curiosity?
I suppose you forgot, in your ego fit of rage,
carelessness only crafts mediocrity.

you can lose your muse each time you refuse
to cherish or respect her.
you can lose your pen
when you don't write or send
your message with conscious clarity.

but I have no worries,
you see, I'm a creator too,
and I know every lie
you paint about me
only colors you.

## TO MY INNER LITTLE GIRL

I want to love you
in all the ways
the others forget to
but some days,
it just doesn't
come easy.
these days,
I'm not afraid
to stand up for you.
I will not cage your rage
because I know
how much it takes for you
to reach that boiling point,
so when you do,
you can trust
I won't abandon you
but I'm still learning
how to speak
more kindly to you,
let you eat
what, when,
and however much
(or little)
you want to
without guilt,
that relentless force
I battle so hard against
to protect you.
by now,
I've learned how to treat you,

to pleasure you,
to make you feel special,
remembered,
considered,
and all that's left
is to convince you
that you really are beautiful,
that the beauty you know lies within
really does shine through
even when
you're convinced it doesn't,
so I will let you be
as quiet or loud
as you are
rather than shaming you
because I know
how raw and vulnerable
you are
and I remind you
of all you are
when you accidentally believe
what they told you,
forgetting that
they don't know you
like I do.
I do love you
imperfectly, but
I am still learning
and not because I have to,
because I want to.

# I AM A GOAT MOTHER.

most days begin with the slow caress—
his warm thumb across my cheek
and back again.

I wake about three,
in the silk of his arms
but my favorite part is when
we get to tell our dreams.

if we're lucky,
the kids sleep in, silent
until we step outside,
where shells crunch beneath our feet
and dirt sand flicks, sticks
between the toes

as we hurry to the metal gate
where six rectangular pupils gaze
back, as wild meets wild,
and I grind my teeth,
begging him to match their bleats

and if I can just stop kissing
the crevices behind their ears
long enough to remember,
I'll grab a square of peanut hay
while goat daddy fills the mineral tray
with alfalfa, seeds, and salt
before we smush their little faces,
give them scratches

then spit
out
the black hairs
that stuck to our lips,
closing the gate,
and walking away

from the fading cries of three—
our sweetest harmony.

# THE WOMAN WHO LOVED HIM

sometimes I think about
the woman who loved him before—
how like me, she might be
sitting now, somewhere on a couch
beside a man she'll never love as much
as the one I got, the one she lost,
that she still thinks about

and we're both watching a screen,
but hers brainwashes her into submission,
enslaves her to a life that isn't her own
(it's called religion).
she envies me, tries desperately
to believe she can put me down.
she's too scared to see
she can also be free.
all she's lost
can still be found.

though, truthfully, I can't hate her,
even if I were to try
and she doesn't know that I think about her
sometimes, when he and I fight,
that I don't see her as the crazy ex
when I think of the whole truth
because I know what loving and fighting hard
can do to someone like you,
someone like me,
someone like us

but you can't really love someone
if you do not love them free.
I'm convinced I'm a better lover
not because of brains or beauty,
or body—
because trust me, you've got it all.

all except my heart, because
I won't leave me out of my own love.

# I WISH TO BE LOVED MADLY

so please do not come to me
if you're not in love with all of me—
the cracks and the crevices,
the art that is the whole of me.

be ready to rake when the leaves fall
and willing to wait,
to hold the child in me
when she can't stand—only crawl.

do not throw me to the wind
or bury me in a grave
that you only plan to visit
too damn little too late.

kaileia suvannamaccha

## WHO LOVES THE LOVER?

there it is—the ache,
the pain I can't escape.

though I try my best to translate,
I wear the worst above my waist—
a bloody stain
I can't erase.

it steals my hunger
like a bad dream
from when I was younger.

it cuts
like a blade in the wrist,

it drags
like your nails on my hips,

forces me to sit
rather than shift.

a whole fetus
overcooked,
unable to be delivered

yet I fear
if I stay here,
the only way it's coming out
is if I tear

and I know
I've been leaking
for years—
always speaking,
but the words just fall
on deaf ears.

tell me, who heals the healer
when they're sick?

who mothers the mother?

then, when her heart is aching,
breaking,
tell me
who loves the lover?

## CLOSURE

in a perfect world,
you come home to me.
nestled in your arms,
you hold me as I cry
and feel my heart ache
inside your own,
maybe for the first time.
you wipe my face,
trace my cheeks in soft kisses,
and in a loving tone, whisper
*you deserve nothing less than my best*
and this time, you mean every word.
*I am here*
you would say.
*everything else can wait,*
*but I will not keep you*
*waiting for me any longer.*

*rebel for love*

I find myself
caught in between
the person you expect me to become
and the person I know
I can only keep suppressing for so long.

## UNMASKED

face the mirror and search for
a reflection that isn't there.
the one you see is the one that's too
hard for them to bear.
restless wanderer, calm your own soul
since you do not allow the others in.
once your apparition is no longer faded,
welcome yourself back to living.
rejuvenated spirit,
open your heart to feeling.
soar above your bones
and detach from this earth.
at last, you are free
to spread your wings.

she used to be good
at reading their scripts
until she started writing
her own.

# PURGE

I don't subscribe to your bullshit advice
*that's just how men are.*
I'm not lowering my standards.
I'm not backing down
when I've already come this far.
you think I haven't seen
where the path of settling leads?

go *distract* myself from difficult feelings?
go on and *wait* to dream a *new* dream?
fit in *his* world, speak *his* language?
fuck that shit
and fuck you for saying it.

your standards for me are just stepping stones.
not my destination,
not my home.

fuck family gatherings and obligations.
fuck casseroles.
fuck retinol!
I'll take sunlight, sunspots,
and wrinkles.

I'll take real
over Botox,
over lip fillers,
over lies and blame.
bitch, stay in your lane.

fuck your ship.
I wish I never even boarded it.
keep your cigarettes,
your gummies,
all your numbing.
too tolerating,
too used to distracting.

I came here to feel.
I want to be alive
and by asking me to be like you,
you're asking me to die.

# WHEN THEY TRY TO SILENCE ME,

I will not shave my thorns.
I will grow honest and proud,
wet, wild, and wonderfully loud.
if I censor my truth, I'm selling a lie
so if you want out from under the bus,
give me something better to write about.

## MY KINGDOM, MY RULES.

no more gifts that come with strings!
whether or not you think
they're decorative,
they will choke me.
I will suffocate.
I have been,
so long as I've stayed.
this misery ends today.
I've made up my mind
and maybe it hurts,
but I'm taking right action anyway.

I stare—
ready,
reckless,
free.

I stand—
heart unbound
in a parallel reality.

guilt?
I don't know her.

grief?
haven't seen her.

naked,
barefoot,
now I can sing!

I am no longer sleepwalking.

call to me
from the feet
of the mountains I've climbed.

I won't be coming down.

I dive into the peace
that comes with being present.
I embrace my natural beauty
as a woman, independent
of the obligations and expectations
placed onto me,
remembering what it means in life
to truly be free.

kaileia suvannamaccha

## THE DISPLACED WASP
*after Mary Oliver*

I ask the displaced wasp
with the orange band around her waist,
spiral-dancing in the wind,
rest-waiting on the pavement
only for a moment
before she disappears
into the shade of the jackfruit tree,
*how has the destruction of all you knew created you?*
*where do you go when your home is in ruins?*
*who do you become*
*when you are orphaned by your own kind?*
*were you ever at home there anyway?*
*I promise*
*I will not bury you*
*in my pity.*

*originally published in *Anti-Heroin Chic*

let mother nature have her way with us.
let her feast and flame
on the fuel we gave her.
let her make of us,
at last,
what we've made of her.

# I LEARNED THE HARD WAY
# THAT PITY IS NOT LOVE.

I knew they couldn't, but
they thought they loved me
not knowing
I was fresh out of battle
with scars that still needed healing,
bloody wounds that kept me from feeling
safe, to be all of myself in their presence.

they welcomed me in—
a stray kitten,
a feral thing,
a wild child,
not knowing.

they waited
for domesticity
to take its proper place,
not knowing as I healed,
I would only get stronger
until the starving bird in the golden cage
could not keep quiet any longer.

they wanted
the warmth of the flame
that was,

before I became
the fire.

## SILLY BIRD,

making nests
that resemble
the ones you resent
'til you learn
that a bird
has always been meant
to make nests
for rest,
but is at home
in the sky.
it is why
each bird needs
its own pair of wings
and
the will
to use them
to fly.

# SHELL OF A MAN I ONCE KNEW

you told her you'd give up everything,
told her you found God
just to see your little girl

but you told me to stop writing,
told me to stop speaking,
neglected my inner little girl.

was it easy to pretend I didn't exist?
was any of it true?
that they're the ones you miss
every day?
that you dream about
every night?

because you tell me you hate her,
that she's crazy, she lies,
but so do you

because you call me crazy
and you tell me I lie
whenever I cry—
you don't care to know why.

I saved my tears for you
so no one else had to see.
I kept your anger between me and my poetry

so when you asked me to stop,
it was like asking me to die.

don't you know if this pen stopped moving,
that soon, so would I?

maybe you did.
maybe you knew all along.
maybe I just didn't want to believe it—
I didn't want to be wrong.

she told me you could never love me.
was it her I should have believed?

I see now, it finally exists
somewhere outside of my mind,
the love you're capable of,
the man you've become.
you've changed, but not in time,

and not for me.

# WHEN WE WERE BEAUTIFUL

why did we fail to see it back then?
that we were beautiful even when
valleys and rivers had yet to set in
and deepen the crust that became of our skin?

why did it feel so hard to let loose
before there were any bodies to lose?
dusk simply teased its game of pretend.
dawn's return gleamed no foreseeable end.

those were the days, before eyes lost their light.
a hug, kiss, and sorry could remedy any fight.
there were no rifts deemed irreparable
and distance, for love, seemed inseparable.

## INCOMPATIBILITY

I am in love with a man who doesn't know
he doesn't love me,
who has read my book
but does not speak in poetry.
he sees black and white where I see rainbow.
he sees a reflection
where there are ripples and waves
distorting the truth
that lies underneath.
he does not know the longing I speak of.
he does not feel to the depths that I feel,
or if he does, he does not express it.
for me, he does not cry.
I am in love with a man who searches for me
as soon as he gets home
because he knows I play hide and seek
(in more ways than one),
who cooks me dinner because he's seen
me burn
everything I touch,
and perhaps everyone,
if I ever let them get close enough.

## GOD SHOULD'VE KNOWN

I always wanted him to prove me wrong
but God, should've known
I'm a woman.

I wanted us to be the exception—
love that never bittered,
milk that never soured,
hearts that never shattered,

the only magic that wasn't a trick.

I wanted to keep him
like my word,
like a promise,
like a photograph.

little did I know,
in my wanting,
I already knew
everything
it wasn't and
could never be.

I was
so certain
I'd found my happy ending
but a dear friend once told me
*good can get in the way of better.*

so I carried the rock

you said you would be
for the both of us,
slept with the weight of it on my heart,
thought it could will you to love me
eventually
in all the ways you said you did,
but wouldn't
whenever it came down to it

and it came down to it—

an avalanche from the Great Wall of China,
heart burst,
bleeding out.
only you had the stitches,
the Band-Aids,
the ribcage,
to hold it all,
to put me back together again,
to save us from
the blind man you became
in all your rage.

they always said men were simple creatures,
but God, should've known
I'm a woman.

# MY MOTHER

a potted plant
stripped from her soil of origin,
deprived of key nutrients,
must be transplanted back
in order to flourish again.

a tube in her ass cheek
draining liquid dis-ease
from years spent holding on,
making homes out of people
in places she didn't belong.

my first introduction to love,
my first introduction to pain,
from the inside
somatically inscribed
into my DNA.

a warrior, a survivor,
a lover, a fighter,
a speaker, a writer,
but if I don't relive, just release,
will I be the first
in our line to choose peace?

I purged through my work,
graduated Trustee Scholar,
did everything in my power
not to burden or bother.

then came your stage four cancer
scared the crap out of me.
if I follow in your footsteps,
will that be my destiny?

because I'd rather be free.
I'd rather love me
and selfishly choose health
over family.

but what's a plant with no roots?
an alarm with no snooze?
what isn't a win
when you've got nothing
to lose?

I freed myself hoping I could take you with me.
won't you come with me?
is it too late already?

I'm not ready
to let you go.
you must heal the root.
you must root to rise

and then, gently
fall
like
snow.

## TO MY LONG-LOST BROTHER

I used to blame it on the drugs.
now, I realize it was always you.
they only woke what was already inside of you,
gave life to the demons that reside in you.
that's how I learned I could no longer confide in you
and finally, why I had to say goodbye to you.

*originally published in *Anti-Heroin Chic*

## EVERY HEARTBREAK PALES IN COMPARISON TO LOSING YOU.

you told me
*the purpose is to know where I come from*
but you never said that once you did,
you'd be ready to leave.
I thought you would at least
tell me.

I've been grieving you my whole life,
so knowing you're really gone
is hard to believe.

where are you?
why can't I feel you around?
always lost, only this time
never to be found?

I told you I loved you last
the morning of February 23
after I woke up from a dream
of you dying.

you told me it was symbolic.
*the old, ignorant me has died.*
why aren't you still here then?
I can't help but think it was
a premonition.

I wish we could have gotten more time.
I wish I could hug you one last time.

I wish you would have called to say goodbye.
I know you love me
just like you know I love you.
I have to believe that's true.
I have to think that I could get through to you,
that you didn't plan on leaving so soon.

the last selfie you sent me, I told you
I could see your soul returning to your eyes.
that's why losing you now is such a surprise,
especially after you apologized.

I am looking for you outside the window
of the airplane,
somewhere above the clouds.
I am listening to your music
and the first voicemail I ever saved,
back in 2012,
when you first got locked up
and you called me.
it's been on repeat.

even at 12 years old, I knew not to delete it.

in elementary school, my teacher called home,
said of the wishes we hung on the walls for the class,
mine was sad
because I wrote that I wanted you back.
I wanted us to be a family again.

you got so mad at me.
too embarrassed to see

how much I missed you,
how much I needed you,

my big brother.

you will never leave me.
I won't let you.
I will cling to
anything and everything
I have left
of you

because I don't know
how I'm going to live

without you.

grief carves with ravenous fangs,
making heavy of the empty.
to be light would feel full,
but the hollow heart fails to ignite
in immortal ache,
the echo we call love.

## STONE OR SEA

lately, I am stone or sea.
no in-between.

I can stare at a wall
and feel nothing at all—
the tears I shed
have said it all.

my heart—excavated.
my mind—scattered.
my body—negligible.
my soul—lost.

my spirit,
still searching

for his.

## BABYSITTER BLUES

as I lay here beside a five-year-old girl,
I read her the stories I wrote
in my journals
when I was her age
and as she reads me hers,
a part of me heals.

I am not 24.
I am five
just like her.

then, we write a story together
about magic bananas
based on the story we played pretend earlier

and as full as I am
of gratitude,
I am overwhelmed,
knowing I am her babysitter
who she loves now, but one day,
may not remember.

at least not all of the details, like she still does
each time I pick her up from school.

there is grief
for the part of me
who misses simpler times,
laying in the same bed as my sister—
our dad in the middle,

singing *on top of old smokey*
back when he still cared
or at least, made us believe that he did
like we believed in Santa Claus

and I try to imagine my mother soft
but she's always been
strong.
she had to be,
and so I know I could never be
a mom.

I don't have it in me—
the strength it would take
to fill her shoes.
I am too soft,
too young,
too scared,
laying here with this five-year-old girl.

I remember now
what playdates feel like.
only now, I tire more easily
and know I couldn't do this on the daily,
even though part of me longs for
a little girl just like her
to share a friendship like this with,
forever.

that's the difference.
this isn't forever—
as beautiful and perfect as it is,

as grateful as I am
that babysitting her is a playdate for my inner child—
the part of me that remains me at my core,
when I stare at the glow-in-the-dark stars on the ceiling
or play pretend,
how I still get so lost in it.

the actress in me surrenders to the storyline, every time.
time flies whenever we're
laughing,
dancing,
or singing
princess songs in the car,
windows down,
sunroof open,
drizzling outside
and it's only us at the playground
and that's why
I can climb and slide
and never think twice
about my age

because I know she only sees my soul.
she's five years old
and so am I

until I remember
I no longer have my brother.

my mom,
I think about all of the choices she didn't make.
she stayed

every time her soul wanted to leave.
she stays
even when parts of her own body betray her
and suddenly, I wish I was five
so I could relive everything

before my brother's addiction,
before my sister's transplants,
before my mom's cancer,
before my parents fell out of love,
before I grew up.

I'm not old enough
to let go.

I'll never be able to
bring a child into this world,

knowing how much grief I carry in my heart
that fuels my art.

I used to have a CD player too.
this little girl is more me than I'm used to.
with her, I'm more free than I'm used to.

a child
trapped inside
an adult body.

open heart,
open mind,
pretending most of the time

that I've grown and changed
when deep inside,
I still feel the same.
I still want to play,
and only now that I found someone to play with,
do I realize it,

that when I'm laying on the floor,
staring at a salt lamp
in a yoga studio,
that I'm just as small
and scared
as ever

because one day, my parents will leave this world
and I'll still be their little girl,
aching, longing, grieving.

the memories, when they come,
will remind me of
the best of their love,
and the worst,
and it will hurt
every time.

it will burn
a hole inside
the deepest part of me
to be filled again
each time I remember

life before it was digital.
these moments were pivotal.

home feels like
making believe
out of whatever we have.

that's life's greatest secret.
it's always been

the little things
(and the little ones)

reminding us
we still got it.

kaileia suvannamaccha

## MY DEAR, YOU ARE THE WORLD.

your body—a microcosmic ecosystem,
an orchestral orgasm where every resonance
sings in harmony with your heartbeat.

your mind—a slippery survivalist,
a battle between contours,
the subconscious reflected
in every perception,
every perspective.

this is
your history to rewrite,
your legacy to ignite
in each breath,
each moment.

this world
as you know it
exists only while you're in it,
so own it.
mold it.
rock n' roll it.

do unto life and love as you see fit.
say what you wish and see what becomes of it.

*originally published on *TheUnsealed.com*

## WHEN WOMEN RETREAT,

we see the value in our gifts
without further explanation.
even as waves of guilt and shame seep in,
we are each held by the other without expectation

and I wonder, *is this only in my imagination?*
I listen.
I feel into my own wisdom.

I hesitate to share it.
they don't hesitate to hear it
when I finally summon the courage.

I learn from witnessing—
the space you take is the space you make.
I wasn't made to wait for an invitation.

it's been the most intimate thing—to sing,
to share my poetic verse,
to voice what so often goes unheard,
otherwise, in other worlds.

where the snow falls, the mind clears.
in the cold, I remember
the warmth of my own beating heart.

I see my breath even as I struggle to catch it.
my skin pales, then peels.
like the snake, I shed.

in the dead of winter,
there is no pressure
to perform.

in the presence of great women,
I question, *am I doing enough?*
since I never saw my mother rest,
not even as she slept,

but they remind me
to be,
to still,
to warm,
to thaw
from the inside out,

to watch
and receive
new life.

## ELEMENTAL

I am nature,
not just of her.

a creation that creates,
love that loves,
part of something bigger

and that something bigger is still me,
like the branch is still part of the tree.
we only call it something different
based on how much of it we see

but if there is no isolation,
no separation,
then all there is to see
and be seen
is me.

# THERE ARE NO SAINTS IN THIS WORLD.

every angel I've met had a devil in her.
every hand that held me has let go
and I know
that sometimes, holding on is harder.

it's not always fun to be the fire—
to burn everything you touch.
you can never get close enough.

in your space,
in your element,
you are content

yet the wave always seeks
to rise again
like the flame always seems
to spark from within.

it's the dance with the demons
that you learn to call by name,
just so you can summon them again.

I'm a criminal no one's chasing,
paying debts I never owed,

traded my spine for a stem
and diamonds for a rose.

I chose nature over nurture,
tore the sail right off the boat,

dove into forbidden waters
before I knew if I could float.

I commit

to living my questions,
not your conclusions.

I am engaged

to sovereignty, sensuality,
listening and learning.

I vow

to choose presence over pressure,
reflect without rushing,
observe without judging.

to water the garden within and without,
to tend to the seed before harvesting the sprout.

I divorce

from that which constricts,
that which constrains,

from those who restrict,
and those who restrain.

I do—all that remains.

## FAÇADE

I swear I could love you both
because I already do.
you just didn't know it.

I met a man who could love me
to the depths that were too much for you.
I would not hold it against you that you couldn't.

I would hold your heart
but this time, I'm holding mine.
I've learned not to trust you with it.

all my love for a façade
because you never knew
I could never reveal
all of me to you.
perhaps, it was because
part of me always knew

it was the only way
to stay
with you.

# ALL OF HER IS WELCOME HERE

I will not shame another woman
for sharing the truth
that lives inside her.
I will not ask her to be
anything other than
all that she is.
I shall yell at her red
then cry for her blue.
I will fight for her green
and laugh with her purple too.
I will celebrate her orange
then bask in her yellow,
and still hold space,
more than enough room
for every other shade
of light
she may reflect
until our eyes become the mirrors
through which, we finally see
what it means
to be perfect.

# I'M LOOKING FOR A WOMAN'S LOVE IN EVERY MAN I MEET.

I look for her eyes—
the way she gazes at the one she loves
with sincere admiration,
especially when they're not looking.

I look for her words—
the way she soothes the soul
with her compassionate tone,
the voice that is sharp yet soft
all at once saying exactly what needs to be said
without compromising what you most need to hear.

I look for her heart—
that open-as-air ceaseless flow
of kindness, of wisdom, of strength, of loving
in action, not just in theory.

I look for her hands—
the slow, sensual touch
that knows how to reach
the places deeper than skin,
those most in need of the delicate caress of fingers,
traversing to the rhythm
of her breath, her heart, her thought stream,
her emotional epicenter.

I start to look for a woman's love in every man I meet
every time I stop looking in the mirror.

# I DON'T FOLLOW MY HEART—
# I LEAD WITH IT.

following my heart led me in and out of arms
that didn't know how to hold me.

it led me to men who only saw me in parts,
who didn't know how to love the whole me.

it taught me to second-guess my instincts,
ignore the reasonings in my mind.

following kept me at a distance from my heart
by leaving the rest of me behind.

now, I've come to learn not to follow my heart,
but to lead with it instead,

finding value in what I feel
as well as what's happening in my head.

instead of being dragged on a leash through life,
I'm carving my own path,

and when love shows up, I request it in full,
refusing to settle for half.

## ODE TO MY FINGERS

I like the smell of my fingers
eating food with me,
making love with me,
creating art with me,
and writing poetry with me.

fingers, that
wash my body,
fold my clothes,
wipe my tears,
scratch the itch,
and hold the parts that hurt
when no one else will.

fingers
drive me wherever I want to go,
pull the blankets up when I get cold,
and will inevitably wrinkle as I get old.

my fingers know it all now
dirt, sand, and snow,
salted water, skin, and bone,
and blood.

these fingers will be
forever my greatest loves.

# WORD PLAY

people say I have a way with words.
more like words have their way with me!
they follow the golden thread
that dissolves into my ear holes

and sometimes,
when I cry,
they slide

down my cheeks
in a moment
of insecurity
or ferocity
or curiosity.

my body is their playground.

I watch them
take control of my fingers,
bend me to their will,
bypass my brain
and speak
directly to my heart,
or from it.

words use me as their vessel,
fill me up,
become my only
sustenance.

to say it is strange to admit, but
the only time they come
is when I submit to them.

# FOR INSPIRATION

to the songs that soothe our souls—
birds, who give voice to dust on butterfly wings,
that set flight to hearts that weigh more in life
than this human body can bring

to the women, who hold me in their arms—
mothers whose love gives birth to all others,
their lips, dripping truths we crave to read
in the lies of men that can't, who weren't made to
bleed.

to the love rising from the ashes within me,
turning dust to nectar, nourishing
petals that sprout, even through fallen leaves.

to the mind, that relentless dynamo,
that wonders even as I slumber.

to these hips I have yet to master
how to shake, that I call home.

to these hardy bones
I fear to break, that I know one day will
wither away.

to these eyes, I know
take me deeper inside
to the true me, myself, and I
I've always known.

to the one who reads these words—
a reflection, a shadow,
that beneath a fruit tree
already lived and died
longer than you or me,
an extension of interconnection,
sparks that lead us back to one
eternal flame
from which we all light and delight in.

to the hands that type
these words into a device
that may one day enslave me.

to pen and paper
that cramp my hand,
an addictive catharsis
giving semblance to

this life—
this foreign concept,
a system my brain can't think itself free from,
a headache, a heartache, all at once
felt and embraced, yet unbound.

for all of this,
I am grateful.

*originally published in *Unseal Your Gratitude: Poems That Illuminate the Beauty in Life*

# WHAT'S THERE TO WRITE ABOUT BUT LOVE?

sunlight poking through the trees
to sneak a peek at me,
watching shadows dance across my skin.

a sip of water
to keep the flowing
going within.

remembering the many fathers I've had
over the years, come and gone.

my mother, our nature.

oh, how I would, in a second, give birth
if only it could be a baby goat instead of a human,

in the arms of a lover whose tide
intertwines with my moon,
even if he never comes close.

perhaps, I'm only meant to make a legacy out of me
and maybe that's enough.
maybe I'm enough.

I see now—
it's always
all about love.

## SOMETHING I DON'T MOVE, BUT MOVES THROUGH ME

I had told the universe my intention—
to live the most epic love story,
but what to do when it finally arrives?
after repeated prayers,
after patience, dedication,
what to do when it comes bare?
as is, as desired,
rather than in disguise?
no need to unscrew the cork
nor wait for the kettle to boil
when the wine is aged
yet sweeter than ever
and the tea has already been poured
and served,
how am I to graciously accept the invitation?
then again, who am I to righteously decline
the soul-speak, heart-bled
timing of the divine?
beyond boundaries,
beyond constructs of the mind,
it is not the faint whisper of a song
but the beat of a warrior's drum
that I forgot I knew the dance to all along.

he told me
to sip hot tea,
you must siphon the air as you sip.

he taught me
the raw garlic trick—
you just swallow it.

he studied
the fascial system—
raindrops on skin as regulation.

he heard
the words I wasn't saying.

he felt
the song my soul was singing.

he knew
the ache my heart was holding—

and he loved me
anyway.

## WE MUST GET BACK TO THE POETRY.

for you,
I am all ears

but I mustn't have you
at the expense
of my words.

a meteor flashes
twice
before my eyes—
fades,
then falls.

give me
all. your. sweet.

another slice of pear.
another carrot.
another date.

feed me
another melting sunset.

kaileia suvannamaccha

sometimes, we write the poetry.
other times, we live it.

# PERSIST

all it took was one dance,
and the brush of our hands,
and the want to kiss without the will
to leave the farm just for the thrill
of the wind in my hair.

all it took was one ride
and the scent of a neck
to know you were mine, even though
I could never let myself have you

because Gregory David Roberts says
*a dream is a place where a wish and a fear meet*
so here comes everything I ever desired
yet I've never been so afraid
to meet my fate

even though I believe in magic,
even though I've seen the signs for myself,
even though I asked and continue to ask,
I cannot explain us away.

I must investigate.
my curiosity is peaked.
between my heart and stomach,
you live, you breathe.
in you,
I see
me, free

and it could be everything
or it could be nothing.

it could be the last heart string.
it could be a delusion and I could be naïve.
it could set fire to the life I built with careful hands,
and burn the best of me down with it.
it could be the fall before an endless winter.

it could be nothing

or it could be everything

and so it already is

yet I resist,
so you

persist.

## SUMMONING

I want you, lilac
painting with old makeup brushes,
playing dress up at home
alone.

the one who breaks
open—
bleeds
golden.

the one they call too much,
the one they don't
call
enough,
I call you back
to launch me forward.

I want you, thorns,
only to love you free.
I want your
*do not forget* lists,
your confessions,
obsessions,
the depth of your love
and all of its lessons.

I want you, freckles
laughing 'til your stomach burns
again,
somehow.

I want you to have
but for once, not be had—
swimming nude
in a world of one's own.

I want your space,
your sovereignty.
I want your forgiveness,
faith,
honesty.

I want you,
sunset in the chest,
singing

(forget who may be listening).

I want you

audacious,
salacious,
ever-so-gracious,

barefoot,
bare-faced,
wave after wave,

I want

all of you.

*rebel for love*

I cried the first time I saw blood between my legs.
I never wanted to become a woman
because I saw my mother that way—
a willing slave, trapped
in the name of marriage and motherhood
and I wanted to stay

a girl
because I still wanted to be free
until I grew up and into the whole of me—

a woman
who chooses not to be caged.

## SIN

I confess no sins,
for these lips
have not missed—
only made—
their mark.
some might call it
a mistake.
I call it
making art.

I am my mother's daughter,
and still my own.
I serve from an underwater throne.
crowned double princess,
both Celtic and Thai,
this mermaid witch
knows how to swim
as well as when to fly.

I am a mourning dove with no name,
swallowed by the crow before I hatched.

now, I see blue shimmers
where they see black feathers,
yet our eyes are the same.

if these wings were made for flying,
why does it feel like dying?
the faster I fall,

earth below my belly,
barely floating,
not yet ready
to be carried
by the breeze.

still, part of me knows
what lies inside
the eye of the storm.

## REBEL FOR LOVE

my mother didn't get cancer
so you could shut me up.
my mother got cancer,
so I learned to speak up.

my mother wasn't beaten
so you could kick me down.
my mother was beaten,
so I learned to stand my ground.

my mother wasn't abandoned
so you could take me or leave me.
my mother was abandoned,
so you will choose me or lose me.

my mother once told me
I came into this world
to teach her about loving.

I didn't come into this world
not to be loving, not to forgive,
not to give or take second chances
worth giving or taking.

I came in love,
so I must be loving.

my mother loved me,
so I must be loved.

# ACKNOWLEDGMENTS

Firstly and forever, thank you to my mother, whose achingly expansive heart inevitably textures my own.

Cyndi Buchanan and Marina Vongphachanh of the Stardust Goddess Alliance, for your sisterhood in co-creation at our weekly open mic poetry nights, and beyond.

The local and online creative communities to which I belong, for your existence and warm embrace.

The poets, especially Janne Robinson and Chelsie Diane, whose authenticity radiates wild permission and inspiration for women like myself to do the same.

My greatest loves and deepest heartbreaks, for exploring the depth and possibilities of human connection with me through our divinely timed reflections in this lifetime.

My brother—a rebel in his own right, whose love reigns eternal.

My heart, for enduring.

*Author Portrait by Matthew Troyer*

# ABOUT THE AUTHOR

Kaileia Étaín Melusine Suvannamaccha, also known as *The Princess Poetess*, is a published literary artist and certified therapeutic art and writing coach, guided by the philosophy of leading with her heart rather than merely following it.

For her, love is a process of inclusion, whereby "the heart knows no other." As a rebel for love, she ponders the core question: "What love are you in if you leave yourself out?"

A Trustee Scholar, she earned her BFA in Creative Writing with minors in Fine Arts and Business from Ringling College of Art and Design in 2022.

Her raw, reflective writing—including poetry and short stories—has appeared in both print and online publications, such as *The Unsealed* and *Sarasota SCENE Magazine*.

Her work "reveals the beauty in vulnerability." She "entrusts the reader with the role of confidant and it proves a worthy endeavor" (Independent Book Review).

*Rebel For Love* is her second poetry collection, following her debut, *In Time I See*, published in 2023.

*@theprincesspoetess*

## ABOUT THE BOOK

*Rebel For Love* is the raw, heartfelt story of a woman who refused to be left out of her own love—a radical exploration of the intersections between fear and desire.

A layered blend of tenderness and tension, these poems and poetic fragments illuminate the dissonance between the fantasy of intimacy and its embodied reality.

At its core, this eclectic collection invites readers to accept, forgive, and transcend the shadows of self-abandonment and self-sabotage in relationships.

Compiled from new and old journals alike—some titled, others not—the book's structure is as rebellious as its contents, mirroring the non-linear paths and patterns found through love, loss, and longing.